ACKNOWLEDGEMENTS

Special thanks to God, firstly, for the inspiration and for giving me the skills to be able to complete this project.

Secondly, I want to thank my husband Shurland and my son Shaquille, for their patience and understanding while completing this book. Ms. Selma Henry, the teacher in my first vegetarian cookery class, for her insight and Mrs. Catherine Spooner for always willingly sharing her knowledge with me.

Finally, I want to thank two other special persons: Dale Callender for his encouragement and Ryan Nurse for believing in me and for his genuine assistance. I could not have done this without any of you.

FINE DINING *Caribbean* VEGETARIAN RECIPES

Kelly's Kitchen

KELLY HENRY

LMH

First Edition

10 9 8 7 6 5 4 3 2 1

All LMH titles, imprints and distributed lines are available at special quantity discounts for bulk purchases for sales promotion, premiums, fund-raising, educational or institutional use.

Cover design: Sanya Dockery
Typeset & book layout: Sanya Dockery
Photography: Wayne Lewis Photography

Published by: LMH Publishing Limited

Suite 10 -11
Sagicor Industrial Park
7 Norman Road
Kingston C.S.O., Jamaica

Tel.: (876) 938-0005; Fax: (876) 759-8752
Email: lmhbookpublishing@cwjamaica.com
Website: www.lmhpublishing.com

Printed in China ISBN: 978-976-8245-44-1

NATIONAL LIBRARY OF JAMAICA CATALOGUING-IN-PUBLICATION DATA

Henry, Kelly
Fine dining Caribbean vegetarian recipes / Kelly Henry

pages ; illustrations ; cm

ISBN 978-976-8245-44-1 (pbk)

1. Vegetarian cooking – Caribbean Area
2. Cookbooks – Caribbean Area
I. Title

641.5636 - dc 23

TABLE OF CONTENTS

APPETIZERS

1 large pineapple
3 large apples
3 large oranges
½ watermelon
1 large bunch of grapes

Preparation time: 20 mins
Serves: 2 – 4 persons

CARIBBEAN FRUIT PLATTER

- Wash and slice fruit.
- Arrange slices on a large platter using the colours of the fruit to create a decorative plate.

TIP. A variety of fruits that are in season may be used.

SOY PATTIES

- 2 cups ground soy beans
- 2 eggs
- 1 onion, minced
- ¼ cup breadcrumbs
- 1 sprig celery, minced
- 1 cup cooked rice
- Salt to taste
- Local fresh seasonings –
  3 stalks chives, chopped; 1 small sweet pepper, chopped; 1 sprig marjoram, chopped; 1 sprig thyme, chopped; 2 tsp dried oregano, 2 tsp paprika, 2 tsp curry
- 2 tsp/10ml soy sauce

Preparation time: 10 mins
Cooking time: 50 mins
Serves: 2 – 4 persons

- Mix soy beans and cooked rice together.
- Add onion, soy sauce, celery and local seasonings to the mixture.
- Whisk the eggs and add to the mixture.
- Slowly add the breadcrumbs to make sure the mixture is pliable.
- Preheat oven to 300°F/149°C.
- Form into patties and bake for 35 minutes or until golden brown.
- Serve in burger buns or as desired.

TIP: Soy beans may be replaced with lentil, chick or split peas.

JAMAICAN SWEET POTATO FRITTERS

2 cups cooked sweet potato
1 cup flour
1 tsp/5g baking powder
2 tsp/10g salt
1 medium-sized onion, chopped fine
2 tsp/10g nutmeg
1 egg, lightly beaten
1 sprig thyme
1 escallion
1 cup water
Oil for frying

Preparation time: 10 mins
Cooking time: 20 mins
Serves 2 – 4 persons

- Combine the cooked sweet potato with the flour, baking powder, onion, thyme, nutmeg, escallion, egg and salt.
- Add enough water to the dry ingredients to make dough pliable and soft.
- Drop small spoonfuls into frying pan and fry on each side until golden brown.
- Serve hot with a dip.

TIP. A sour cream and yogurt dipping sauce would work well.

BAJAN STUFFED EGGS WITH VEGETABLE FILLING

- Cut the hard boiled eggs in half.
- Remove the yolks and place in a large bowl.
- Puree the carrot, sweet corn and green peas.
- Put the pureed mixture in the bowl with the yolks.
- Add the finely minced onion to the mixture.
- Add salt to taste.
- Scoop small portions of the vegetable filling and place in the hard boiled eggs.
- Decorate with a sprig of parsley.
- Serve at room temperature.

4 large eggs, hard boiled
1 large carrot
1 small onion, finely minced
½ cup of sweet corn
Salt to taste
½ cup of green peas
2 sprigs parsley

Preparation time: 10 mins
Cooking time: 20 mins
Serves: 2 – 4 persons

LENTIL BALLS

1 cup lentils
2 medium-sized potatoes
1 onion, minced
¼ cup breadcrumbs
1 sprig celery, minced
1 sweet pepper, finely chopped
Salt to taste
Local fresh seasonings – 3 stalks chives, chopped; 1 small sweet pepper, chopped; 1 sprig marjoram, chopped; 1 sprig thyme, chopped; 2 tsp dried oregano, 2 tsp paprika, 2 tsp curry
2 tsp soy sauce
½ cup flour
3 tbsp/44ml cooking oil
2 eggs
¼ cup milk

Preparation time: 20 mins
Cooking time: 30 mins
Serves: 4 – 6 persons

- Cut potatoes in large squares and cook with lentils in large saucepan.
- When cooked, mash the potatoes and lentils together, adding the onion, soy sauce, sweet pepper, celery and local seasonings to the mixture.
- Use the mixture to form equally sized balls with your hands.
- Prepare the egg batter by whisking the egg and adding the milk.
- Combine flour and breadcrumbs on a large plate.
- Dip the lentil balls into the egg batter, then roll them in the flour and breadcrumbs mixture; and deep fat fry until golden brown.
- Serve hot.

'MEATBALLS' WITH GUAVA AND GINGER SAUCE

2 cups soy mince or granburger
2 eggs
1 medium-sized onion, minced
½ cup breadcrumbs
1 sprig celery, minced
1 sweet pepper, finely chopped
Local fresh seasonings – 3 stalks chives, chopped; 1 small sweet pepper, chopped; 1 sprig marjoram, chopped; 1 sprig thyme, chopped; 2 tsp dried oregano, 2 tsp paprika, 2 tsp curry
2 tsp/10ml soy sauce
Salt to taste
Oil for frying

Preparation time: 10 mins
Cooking time: 25 mins
Serves 4 – 6 persons

- Soak soy mince or granburger in seasoned hot water for fifteen minutes.
- Strain soy mince or granburger and add onion, sweet pepper, soy sauce, celery and mix evenly.
- Whisk eggs and add to the mixture, stirring in breadcrumbs until the mixture is pliable.
- Form into small balls. Dip in egg batter and roll in breadcrumbs.
- Fry until golden brown.

GINGER SAUCE

4 ripe guavas
1 onion, minced
2 tsp dried oregano
2 tsp paprika
2 tsp curry
¼ cup of minced ginger
1 sweet pepper, minced
2 tbsp/1oz corn starch
2 tbsp/1oz of butter

- Blend guavas and ginger together.
- Sauté onion, sweet pepper.
- Add seasonings, then the blended guava and ginger mixture.
- Stir well, then add the corn starch to create a thickness.

1 medium-sized pumpkin
2 tsp soy sauce
1 small potato
Salt to taste
1 large onion, diced
1 egg
1 large sweet pepper, diced
1 cup breadcrumbs
Fresh herbs – 1 sprig marjoram, chopped; 1 sprig basil, chopped; 2 stalks chives, chopped
Spices – ½ tsp cinnamon, ½ tsp nutmeg

Preparation time: 10 mins
Cooking time: 25 mins
Serves 4 – 6 persons

PUMPKIN FRITTERS

- Cook pumpkin and potato in lightly seasoned water.
- When cooked, mash in a large bowl.
- Add diced onions, sweet pepper and mix well.
- Add fresh herbs, spices, and soy sauce to the mixture and salt to taste.
- Whisk egg until light and fluffy.
- Form small patties with mixture. Dip into egg mixture and roll in the breadcrumbs.
- Deep fry until golden brown.
- Serve hot.

CUCUMBER CUPS

- Cut cucumbers into 1-inch chunks.
- Shape the chunks into small cups with the base smaller than the top.
- Scoop out centers of cucumber with a melon baller making cucumber cups, leaving ¼ -inch walls.
- Salt lightly, turn upside down on paper towels to drain while you make the filling.

FILLING

- In a small bowl combine grated cheese, diced celery, mayonnaise, sweet pepper, onion, salt and pepper.
- Fill each cup with the filling. Garnish with celery leaves and serve.

2 large cucumbers
6 celery leaves
½ cup cheese, finely grated
3 tsp/15g green onion, thinly sliced
¼ cup celery, finely diced
Salt & pepper to taste
1-½ tbsp/.75oz mayonnaise

Preparation time: 7 mins
Cooking time: 20 mins
Serves 4 – 6 persons

1 cup plain flour
2 tbsp/30ml vegetable oil
2 tsp salt
80 ml warm water

Preparation time: 7 mins
Cooking time: 1hr 20 mins
Serves 4 – 6 persons

1 potato, finely diced
1 onion, finely chopped
1 carrot, finely diced
1 cup frozen peas
2 cloves crushed garlic
Salt and pepper to taste
1 tbsp vegetable oil
½ cup of vegetable stock
2 tsp curry powder

VEGETABLE SAMOSA

- Mix flour and salt into a bowl. Make a well into the centre and add the oil and enough water to make a firm dough.
- Knead dough on a floured surface until smooth and roll into a ball.
- Cover in plastic wrap and set aside at room temperature for 20 minutes.
- Divide pastry into 12 equal pieces. Roll each piece into a ball and roll out into a circle of 15 cm.
- Divide this circle into two equal pieces with a knife, brush each edge with a little water and form a cone shape around your fingers, sealing the dampened edge.
- Fill the cases with a tablespoon of vegetable stock and press the two dampened edges together to seal the top of the cone.
- Deep fry the samosas in hot oil until crisp and brown. Take out and drain on a paper towel.

FILLING

- Heat oil in a frying pan. Add the onion and garlic, mix in the spices and fry until soft.
- Add vegetables, seasoning and stir well until coated.
- Add stock. Cover and simmer for 30 minutes until cooked.

TRINI PHOLORIE

2 cups/1 lb flour
10 leaves culantro (chadon beni), minced
5 small cloves garlic
1 small hot pepper, minced
½ tsp saffron
1 tsp yeast
1 tsp salt
1 cup water
½ tsp baking powder
Oil for frying

Preparation time: 10 mins
Cooking time: 1hr 20 mins
Serves 6 – 8 persons

- Mix flour, yeast and baking powder.
- Add the saffron and salt and mix well.
- In a separate bowl, mix minced culantro leaves, minced hot peppers, garlic and water.
- Add four tablespoons of the mixture to the flour at a time while mixing, until all of the mixture is incorporated.
- Mix to a smooth thick paste and leave to raise for about an hour.
- Heat oil in skillet or frying pan and use large spoon to drop batter to fry.
- Fry until slightly brown.
- Drain and place on paper towels.

Tip: Tumeric powder may be used instead of saffron.

SALADS

1 head lettuce
1 small onion
2 large tomatoes
1 large green sweet pepper
2 large cucumbers
1 large English apple
Salad dressing (optional)

Preparation time: 15 mins
Serves 4 – 6 persons

TOSSED SALAD WITH APPLE

- Shred the lettuce leaves.
- Dice the cucumbers and tomatoes.
- Make onion rings and chop the sweet peppers.
- Grate the English apple.
- Toss all the ingredients together in a large bowl.
- Use with salad dressing if desired.

½ head cabbage
1 onion, minced
4 carrots
4 tbsp of mayonnaise
4 tbsp sugar
1 sweet pepper, minced

Preparation time: 15 mins
Serves 4 – 6 persons

COLE SLAW

- Shred cabbage finely.
- Grate the carrots using a grater or food processor.
- Mix all the ingredients together.
- Serve cold.

GUYANESE FOUR-BEAN SALAD

16oz can red kidney beans, drained
1 medium-sized green pepper, chopped
16oz can wax beans, drained
2 tbsp/30g chopped parsley
1 lb boiled soy beans, drained
½ cup salad oil
1 lb boiled blackeye beans, cooked
1 cup vinegar
1 medium-sized onion, thinly sliced and separated into rings
1 cup sugar
½ tsp dry mustard
1 tsp salt
½ tsp dried tarragon leaves, crushed
½ tsp dried basil leaves, crushed

Preparation time: 15 mins
Serves 4-6

- Combine the beans, pepper and onion in a bowl.
- In a separate bowl, thoroughly mix the sugar, vinegar, oil, parsley, salt, mustard, tarragon and basil together.
- Pour this dressing mixture over the vegetables and stir.
- Cover and chill thoroughly.
- Stir the salad occasionally while it is being chilled.
- Just before serving, stir again and drain.

POTATO SALAD

6 large potatoes
1 onion, minced
2 hard boiled eggs
15oz can mixed vegetables
4 tbsp/2oz mayonnaise
Salt to taste

Preparation time: 15 mins
Cooking time: 15 mins
Serves 4 – 6 persons

- Boil potatoes in skin.
- Drain and let cool.
- Peel the skin off the potatoes using a potato peeler or paring knife.
- Dice potatoes and add onion and mixed vegetables.
- Add the mayonnaise and blend well.
- Add the grated hard boiled egg and mix lightly.
- Serve cold.

Tip: **Green bananas may also be used instead of potatoes (St. Lucia).**

VEGETABLE SALAD

4 large carrots
1 head cabbage
1 large cucumber, grated
1 small onion
Juice from one lime
1 lb tomatoes
Salt to taste
1 head lettuce

Preparation time: 20 mins
Serves 4 – 6 persons

- Grate the carrots and cabbage together in a large bowl.
- Blend with salt and lime juice.
- Peel cucumber, mark the sides and dice moderately.
- Arrange the salad attractively on a salad platter.

PICKLED GLUTEN

2 steaks gluten
1 lime, juiced
1 large cucumber, grated
1 large onion, chopped
1 large sweet pepper, chopped
1 sprig or parsley, chopped
2tsp salt
1 ripe golden apple, grated (optional)

Preparation time: 20 mins
Serves 4 – 6 persons

- Mix the cucumber, onion, sweet pepper and parsley together in a bowl.
- Chop the gluten and add to the mixture.
- Add the grated golden apple for extra tangy flavor (optional).
- Pour the lime juice and add a pinch of salt.
- Serve cold.

SOUPS

SPICY CORN CHOWDER

3 tbsp/44g flour
4 tbsp/2oz butter
1 cup/8oz milk
1 large onion, chopped
14oz can creamed corn
1 large sweet pepper, chopped
Local seasonings – 3 stalks chives, chopped; 1 small sweet pepper, chopped; 1 sprig marjoram, chopped; 1 sprig thyme, chopped; 2 tsp dried oregano, 2 tsp paprika, 2 tsp curry
1 tsp white pepper

Preparation time: 15 mins
Cooking time: 20 mins
Serves 4 – 6 persons

- Sauté onion and sweet pepper until tender.
- Add flour until it becomes a paste-like consistency.
- Add milk and seasonings and boil for five minutes.
- Add creamed corn and cook for another five minutes.
- Serve hot.

SPLIT PEA SOUP

- 1 cup split peas
- 1 large onion, chopped
- 1 large sweet pepper
- 1 stalk celery
- Salt to taste
- 2 tsp soy sauce
- Fresh herbs – 1 sprig marjoram, chopped; 1 sprig basil, chopped; 2 stalks chives, chopped
- 1 large potato, cubed
- 1 sweet pepper, chopped

Preparation time: 15 mins
Cooking time: 20 mins
Serves 4 – 6 persons

- Cook the split peas in highly seasoned water, using all the herbs.
- Add cubed potatoes.
- When the potatoes are half-way cooked, add onions, sweet pepper, celery, soy sauce, and salt to taste.
- Bring to boil.
- Serve hot.
- Serve with garlic bread or croutons.

VEGETABLE SOUP

1 large English potato
2 large onions
1 medium-sized sweet potato
1 large sweet pepper
2 large carrots
3 large beets
Fresh herbs – 1 sprig marjoram, chopped; 1 sprig basil, chopped; 2 stalks chives, chopped
2 tsp soya sauce
1 large celery stick

Preparation time: 10 mins
Cooking time: 25 mins
Serves 4 – 6 persons

- Add all the ingredients together in a medium-sized saucepan.
- Allow to boil until vegetables are cooked.
- Season the pot with all herbs.
- Serve hot with garlic bread or croutons.

Tip: Other vegetables are optional.

PUMPKIN SOUP

4 cups chopped pumpkin
1 sweet pepper, chopped
1 large onion, chopped
1 stalk celery, chopped
Salt to taste
2 tsp soya sauce
1 large potato, cubed
1 tbsp/15g cooking oil
Fresh herbs – 1 sprig marjoram, chopped; 1 sprig basil, chopped; 2 stalks chives, chopped; 1 sprig oregano, chopped; 1 sprig parsley, chopped
Dried herbs – ½ tsp paprika, ½ tsp curry

Preparation time: 15 mins
Cooking time: 20 mins
Serves 4 – 6 persons

- To a large sauce pan of boiling water, add cooking oil, a pinch of salt and the fresh and dried herbs; add the pumpkin and potatoes and cook until tender.
- Add a dash of dried herbs and finely chopped fresh herbs.
- Add onions, sweet pepper, celery, soy sauce and salt to taste.
- Bring to boil.
- Cool slightly.
- In small batches, transfer to food processor and blend until smooth.
- Return to heat, bring to boil again.
- Serve hot with garlic bread or croutons.

CREAM OF ONION SOUP

2 onions, finely chopped
½ tsp salt
4 tbsp/2oz butter
½ cup/4oz flour
14oz can vegetable broth
1 large can evaporated milk
1½ cup water
½ tsp thyme
2 bay leaves

Preparation time: 15 mins
Cooking time: 25 mins
Serves 4 – 6 persons

- Sauté onions in butter until tender.
- Mix flour and vegetable broth and add to onion mixture.
- Add milk, water, and other ingredients.
- Cook slowly for 20 minutes.
- Puree in blender and serve hot with garlic bread or croutons.

2 cups vegetable stock
8-10 string beans, chopped
1 large onion, minced
½ tsp black pepper
1 sweet pepper, chopped
1 ½ cups/12oz chopped callaloo
Fresh herbs -1 sprig marjoram, chopped; 1 sprig basil, chopped; 2 stalks chives, chopped
½ cup/4oz chopped okra
2 tbsp/1oz ketchup
Salt to taste

Preparation time: 10 mins
Cooking time: 20 mins
Serves 2-4 persons

CALLALOO SOUP

- Remove the thick stems from the callaloo leaves and chop the leaves.
- Put vegetable stock, onion, sweet pepper and fresh herbs in large saucepan.
- Add the chopped callaloo, ketchup, black pepper and salt to taste.
- Allow to simmer for about ten minutes.
- Add the okra and string beans and cook for another 5 minutes.
- Remove from stove, puree in blender or food processor.
- Return to heat and adjust seasonings. Serve hot.

MAIN COURSES

STARCHES

PINEAPPLE SWEET POTATO

4-5 lbs sweet potatoes
Sugar to taste
14 oz can crushed pineapple
1 cup milk
4 pineapple rings
4 tbsp/2oz margarine

Preparation time: 20 mins
Cooking time: 1 hr
Serves 4 – 6 persons

- Preheat oven to 350°F/177°C for five minutes before using.
- Peel and dice potatoes, cook until soft.
- Mash potatoes and add the crushed pineapple.
- Add margarine and enough milk to make it smooth.
- Sweeten to taste.
- Place the sweet potato in a greased dish and decorate with pineapple rings.
- Bake for 45 minutes.

4 cups rice
2 tbsp/1oz cooking oil
1 celery stick
1 sweet pepper, chopped
2 large carrots, grated
1 large onion, minced
2 cups cabbage, shredded finely
Local seasonings – 3 stalks chives, chopped; 1 sprig marjoram, chopped; 1 sprig thyme, chopped; 2 tsp dried oregano, 2 tsp paprika, 2 tsp curry
2 large beets, chopped
14oz can mixed vegetables
Salt to taste

Preparation time: 20 mins
Cooking time: 35 mins
Serves 4 – 6 persons

VEGETABLE RICE

- Boil water, add rice with oil and seasonings.
- Salt to taste.
- Sauté celery, carrots, cabbage and beets together, then add onion and sweet pepper.
- Add local seasonings.
- Mix cooked rice together evenly with vegetables in a little water.
- Add can of mixed vegetables and allow to simmer on slow heat. Serve hot.

Tip: Vegetables can be replaced with any type of cooked peas.

BRAWTA
Breadfruit

Breadfruit is a staple food in many tropical regions. Before being eaten, they are roasted, baked, fried or boiled. When cooked, the taste is described as potato-like, or similar to freshly baked bread. Nutritional analysis reveals that breadfruit is a relatively good source of iron, calcium, potassium, riboflavin and niacin. The mature fruit is high in carbohydrates, low in fat and protein, and a good source of minerals and vitamins, especially B vitamins. The nutritional composition of breadfruit varies depending on the method of preparation and the ripeness of the breadfruit (ripe breadfruit is more nutritious).

Breadfruit is a cook's delight. It can be cooked and eaten at all stages of maturity, although it is most commonly harvested and consumed when it is mature but firm. It can be used in place of potato and as a rice substitute. The very green ones are used for chips when the breadfruit is green, but mature; the riper, but firm, ones can be used for pie in much the same way as macaroni and cheese. It can be roasted with butter on an open fire and can be boiled as a simple side dish. It also makes a good soufflé when combined with milk and eggs, and can be made into a roll with stuffing. It can be boiled and crushed, mixed with seasonings to make a pie. Breadfruit must be used within a few days of being picked.

It is often stored in water to prevent it from deteriorating.

SPICY BREADFRUIT PIE

- Preheat oven at 350°F/177°C for 15 minutes.
- Allow soya mince to soak in hot seasoned water for 45 minutes.
- Cut breadfruit into quarters and cook.
- Make a cheese sauce: Sauté onion and sweet pepper and add cheese and ketchup and white pepper.
- Add breadfruit to cheese sauce and mash on low heat, adding milk and butter until creamy.
- For filling: Sauté onion and sweet pepper, adding soya mince and all other seasonings.
- Put half of breadfruit mixture in a greased baking dish.
- Add a layer of spicy soya mince.
- Cover with other half of breadfruit.
- Top up with breadcrumbs and bake for 45 minutes.

Tip: **Season water by adding chopped onion, sweet pepper, bouquet garni and a pinch of salt.**

1 large, firm breadfruit
1 cup grated cheese
1 cup breadcrumbs
1 large onion
1 large sweet pepper
½ tsp white pepper
1 cup milk
3 tbsp/44g butter
½ tsp cayenne pepper
Local seasonings – 3 stalks chives, chopped; 1 small sweet pepper, chopped; 1 sprig marjoram, chopped; 1 sprig thyme, chopped; 2 tsp dried oregano; 2 tsp paprika; 2 tsp curry
½ cup mustard
2 cups soya mince
3 tbsp/44g ketchup

Preparation time: 45 mins
Cooking time: 1 hr 15 mins
Serves 4 – 6 persons

COU-COU

6 okras, thinly sliced
1 tbsp butter
2 cups cornmeal
2 cups cold water
1 tsp salt
1 small onion, minced

Preparation time: 10 mins
Cooking time: 30 mins
Serves 8-10 persons

- Cook the okras in boiling water with salt and onion until soft.
- Mix the cornmeal in cold water to a smooth paste.
- Add the cornmeal paste to the boiling water, stirring constantly with a 'cou-cou stick' (wooden spoon).
- When the mixture becomes stiff and firm, the cou-cou is ready.
- Serve hot.

STEAMED PUDDING

- Preheat oven to 350°F/177°C for five mintes before use.
- Grate sweet potatoes in a bowl.
- Add thyme, red pepper, sweet marjoram, margarine, salt to taste, coloring, sugar, and clove powder.
- Add water to these ingredients to make mixture of a loose consistency.
- Bake for 45 minutes and serve hot.

1 tbsp coloring
4 tbsp margarine
1 tbsp clove powder
2 lbs/32oz sweet potato
1 sprig thyme
1 red pepper
1 sprig sweet marjoram
¼ cup sugar
Salt to taste

Preparation time: 10 mins
Cooking time: 1 hr 10 mins
Serves 4 – 6 persons

POTATO CASSEROLE

6 large sliced potatoes
1 onion, minced
14oz can mushrooms
1 sweet pepper, minced
3 cups/24oz soya mince
½ tsp cayenne pepper
1½ cups of grated cheese
Herbs – ½ tsp curry,
½ tsp paprika,
½ tsp thyme,
½ tsp marjoram,
½ tsp basil,
½ tsp oregano
2 tbsp ketchup

Preparation time: 15 mins
Cooking time: 1 hr
Serves 4 – 6 persons

(SOYA MINCE SAUCE)

- Sauté onion, sweet pepper and soya mince together.
- Add herbs, cayenne pepper and ketchup until tasty.
- Add a little water but maintain thickness.

(MAIN DISH)

- Preheat oven to 350°F/177°C.
- Grease a large dish.
- Put a layer of sauce in the dish.
- Cover sauce with a layer of sliced potatoes.
- Place a layer of grated cheese on potatoes.
- Place a layer of mushroom cream on the cheese.
- Repeat steps 2-4.
- Top off with grated cheese and breadcrumbs mixed.
- Bake for 45 minutes and serve hot.

BAKED STUFFED POTATOES

- 6 large potatoes
- 14oz can corn
- 1 large onion
- ¼ cup/4oz grated cheese
- 1 sweet pepper
- Fresh seasonings – 3 stalks chives, chopped; 1 sprig marjoram, chopped; 1 sprig thyme, chopped
- Dried seasonings – 2 tsp dried oregano, 2 tsp paprika, 2 tsp curry

Preparation time: 15 mins
Cooking time: 1 hr 15 mins
Serves 4 – 6 persons

- Preheat oven to 300°F/149°C degrees.
- Prick potatoes then bake for 45 minutes.
- Scoop out the inside of the potatoes, leaving the skin intact.
- Sauté the onion, sweet pepper, seasoning and corn together then mix with the potatoes that was scooped out.
- Put the mixture back into the potato skin and cover with grated cheese.
- Bake for appoximately 30 minutes.

CORN DELIGHT

2 cups creamed style corn
1 egg
1 large onion, chopped
1 large sweet pepper, chopped
½ cup/4oz breadcrumbs
½ cup/4oz corn flour
Local fresh seasonings –
1 sprig parsley,
1 sprig marjoram,
1 sprig thyme

Preparation time: 15 mins
Cooking time: 1 hr
Serves 4 – 6 persons

- Preheat oven to 350°F/177°C.
- Whisk egg briskly.
- Add onion, sweet pepper, parsley and fresh seasonings together.
- Mix creamed corn to mixture and blend well.
- Combine the breadcrumbs and corn flour and blend well.
- Place in a greased dish and bake for 45 minutes or until done.
- Serve hot.

BRAWTA
Nuts

Rich in protein, calcium and vitamin E, the almond is a nutritional powerhouse. Incorporate the benefits of almonds into your diet with raw almond cheese, a delicious fermented dish that adds nutrition and flavor to a raw meal. And although it takes some time to make, it's incredibly easy!

MACARONI & NUT PIE

1 large box of macaroni
1 large onion, minced
¼ cup milk
Fresh herbs – 3 stalks chives, chopped; 1 sprig marjoram, chopped; 1 sprig thyme, chopped
2 tbsp/1oz butter
1 sweet pepper, chopped
2 tbsp Ragu vegetable sauce
1 stalk celery
¾ cup breadcrumbs
2 tbsp/1oz cooking oil
1 cup cashew nuts
Salt to taste
Dry seasonings –
½ tsp thyme,
½ tsp curry,
½ tsp paprika,
½ tsp basil,
½ tsp oregano

Preparation time: 20 mins
Cooking time: 45 mins
Serves 6 – 8 persons

- Half cook macaroni with 2 tbsp/1oz of cooking oil and salt to taste.
- When done, put the macaroni in a large colander and rinse with cold water.
- Blend the nuts, adding all the dry and fresh seasonings and herbs, onion and sweet pepper and a little water. Paste should be highly seasoned and very tasty.
- Mix the seasoned nut paste and the macaroni together, adding the Ragu sauce and breadcrumbs.
- Place mixture in a greased baking pan and preheat oven to 300°F/149°C degrees.
- Cover the remaining nut paste on the top and sprinkle breadcrumbs.
- Bake at 375°F/190°C for 30 minutes.

MAIN COURSES

PROTEIN

LENTIL ROAST

2 cups cooked lentil peas
6oz can tomato soup
1 medium-sized onion, minced
2 eggs
Dry breadcrumbs
1 sprig parsley
1 sprig celery, minced
Salt to taste
Local herbs –
½ tsp curry,
½ tsp paprika
½ tsp thyme,
½ marjoram,
½ tsp basil,
½ tsp oregano

Preparation Time: 10 mins
Cooking Time: 45 mins
Serves 6 -8 persons

- Cook and season lentil peas.
- Whisk eggs and add minced onion.
- Mash peas and add all the other ingredients together.
- Preheat oven to 375°F/190°C.
- Blend until tasty.
- Pour into a greased baking dish and bake for 30 minutes.

Tip: Lentil peas can be substituted for any other kind of peas.

BRAWTA
Chickpeas

They're inexpensive and surprisingly good for you. Chickpeas are an excellent addition to the kitchen cabinet, not only because they're healthy, but because they're versatile. Adding chickpeas to soups, salads, as a side dish, or pureeing them into hummus are just a few of the ideas for these popular legumes. What are the health benefits of chickpeas?

Chickpeas (also known as garbanzo beans) provide an excellent source of molybdenum. They are a very good source of folic acid, fiber, and manganese. They are also a good source of protein, as well as minerals such as iron, copper, zinc, and magnesium. As a good source of fiber, they can help lower cholesterol and improve blood sugar levels. This makes them a great food especially for diabetics and insulin-resistant individuals. When served with high quality grains, chickpeas are an extremely low-fat, complete protein food.

CHICKPEA ROAST

2 cups chickpeas, cooked
1 medium-sized onion, minced
1 large potato
1 sweet pepper, minced
1 small squash
2 eggs
2 tbsp/1oz tomato paste
Peanut butter (optional)
Herbs – ½ tsp curry,
½ tsp paprika,
½ tsp thyme,
½ marjoram,
½ tsp basil,
½ tsp oregano

Preparation time: 15 mins
Cooking time: 1 hour
Serves 4 – 6 persons

- Cook potato and squash.
- Mash chickpeas, potato and squash in a large mixing bowl.
- Add all other ingredients and salt to taste.
- Blend until tasty.
- Put into a greased baking dish and bake for approximately 30 minutes at 350°F/177°C or until golden brown.
- Serve slices hot.

BRAWTA
Gluten

Wheat gluten is the water-insoluble protein portion contained within the endosperm of wheat. Gluten can be separated from wheat, with the resulting substance consisting mainly of protein but also containing small amounts of fat, moisture and ash. The protein component of gluten is comprised of many different types of protein molecules, the majority of which fall under the classification of gliadin (single-chained) or glutenin (multi-chained) protein fractions. These proteins give gluten its characteristic cohesive and elastic properties, which serve to make wheat unique in its suitability for bread making.

The storage proteins of wheat are unique because they are also functional proteins. They do not have enzyme activity, but they are the only cereal proteins to form a strong, cohesive dough that will retain gas and produce light baked products. They can be easily isolated by removing starch and albumins/globulins by gently working a dough under a small stream of cold water. After washing, a rubbery ball is left, which is called gluten.

This food is very low in saturated fat, cholesterol and sodium. It is also a good source of selenium, and a very good source of protein.

Gluten is wheat gum, the insoluble component of grains (such as wheat, barley, and rye). It is a mixture of gliadin, glutenin and other proteins. Gluten causes allergy-like reactions in certain people. A gluten-free diet is the primary therapeutic treatment for celiac disease.

Wheat gluten contains approximately 75–80% protein. Thus, its primary nutritional usage is for protein supplementation, with applications in a variety of products, such as cereals and specialty beverages. While wheat gluten is limited in its content of the amino acid lysine, it is still an effective protein fortificant, especially when used in conjunction with soy, a protein source high in lysine. U.S. government regulations allow for fortification of foods with protein (2), and wheat gluten is one of a variety of sources that can be used for this purpose.

8 cups/4lbs flour
3 – 5 cups water

Preparation time: 2 mins
Cooking time: 1½ hours
Serves 8 – 10 persons

GLUTEN

- Make a dough with the flour and water.
- Knead until a smooth texture is obtained.
- Put into cold water and let stand for ½ hour to 1 hour.
- Work the dough steadily with your hands. As it is worked in the water, the starch will wash out.
- As the water becomes milky, pour it off through a strainer and add fresh water.
- Repeat steps 4 and 5 until the water becomes clear.
- You now have a lump of gluten. Cut into steaks and store until ready to use.

4 gluten steaks
½ cup/4oz of olive oil
Dry seasonings –
½ tsp thyme,
½ tsp curry,
½ tsp paprika,
½ tsp basil,
½ tsp oregano
Fresh seasonings – 3 stalks chives, chopped; 1 sprig marjoram, chopped; 1 sprig thyme, chopped
2 tbsp/28g soy sauce

Preparation time: 5 mins
Cooking time: ½ hour
Serves 4 – 6 persons

GLUTEN STEAKS

- Season the gluten with all the dry and fresh seasonings and add the soy sauce. Allow to marinate for ½ hour.
- Heat the olive oil and fry the gluten steaks until golden brown.
- Serve hot.

GLUTEN & VEGETABLE CASSEROLE

1 lb cooked gluten
1 large carrot, grated
½ cup breadcrumbs
3tbsp/42g margarine
1 ripe plantain, finely chopped
1 sprig celery, finely chopped
2 large onions
½ cup Ragu sauce
1 large sweet pepper, chopped
2 tsp seasoned salt
1 glove garlic
½ cup grated cheese

Preparation Time: 20 mins
Cooking Time: 25 mins
Serves 6 – 8 persons

- Preheat oven at 350°F/177°C.
- Slice seasoned gluten thinly.
- Sauté onion, sweet pepper, chopped garlic, grated carrot, ripe plantains and celery. Add seasoned salt and 2 teaspoons of Ragu sauce and stir.
- Grease a casserole dish and put 1 layer of the gluten.
- Spread some Ragu sauce and add a layer of sautéed vegetables.
- Sprinkle a little grated cheese and breadcrumbs.
- Repeat methods 3 to 6.
- Press firmly into casserole dish and bake for 25 minutes.

BRAWTA
Tofu

Tofu, also known as soybean curd, is a soft, cheese-like food made by curdling fresh, hot soymilk with a coagulant. Traditionally, the curdling agent used to make tofu is nigari, a compound found in natural ocean water, or calcium sulfate, a naturally occurring mineral. Curds also can be produced by acidic foods like lemon juice or vinegar. The curds then are generally pressed into a solid block.

Tofu was first used in China around 200 B.C. Although the discovery of the process for making tofu is lost to the ages, Chinese legend has it that the first batch of tofu was created by accident. A Chinese cook added nigari to flavor a batch of pureéd, cooked soy beans, and the nigari produced the curd that we know today as tofu.

In recipes, tofu acts like a sponge and has the miraculous ability to soak up any flavor that is added to it. Crumble it into a pot of spicy chilli sauce and it tastes like chilli. Blend it with cocoa and sweetener and it becomes a double for chocolate cream pie filling. Cubes of firm tofu can be added to any casserole or soup.

STIR FRIED TOFU

½ lb tofu
4 tbsp/2oz fresh parsley, minced
¼ cup cashew pieces
1 tbsp/14g curry powder
1 tbsp/14g cooking oil
1 tbsp/14g soy sauce
1 tbsp/14g fresh ginger, minced
½ cup coconut milk, light or regular
1 - 2 cloves garlic, minced
½ cup water or vegetable stock
½ cup mixed vegetables
½ tsp salt
½ tsp white pepper

Preparation time: 20 mins
Cooking time: 25 mins
Serves 4 – 6 persons

- Cut the tofu into slices about 1– 2 inches and place in a bowl for a few minutes, stir in soy sauce and set aside.
- Heat oil on low in a stir-fry pan, sauté pan or deep skillet.
- Mince the garlic and ginger.
- Add the ginger, garlic, mixed vegetables and cashews to the pan, turn up the heat a bit, and stir fry until the vegetables are slightly cooked and the cashews a little brown.
- Add the curry powder and stir fry briefly.
- Stir in tofu, water and coconut milk. Add salt and pepper to taste.
- Add the parsley, cover and cook on low flame for five minutes to blend the flavors.
- Serve with a starch or vegetable dish.

JAMAICAN CURRY LENTILS

- Soak olive oil, ¼ cup of water, garlic salt and 1 cup lentils in a stew pot overnight.
- Sauté lentils with chopped onion and vegetables.
- Add curry and ½ tsp sea salt to taste and mix until lightly thickened.
- Cook for 10 minutes, adding water to maintain stew.

1 cup dried lentils
Diced vegetables –
1 large carrot,
2 stalks celery,
2 large potatoes
1 onion, chopped
½ tsp garlic salt
½ tsp sea salt to taste
2 tbsp/1oz curry
¼ cup water
2 tbsp/1oz olive oil
4 tbsp/2oz curry

Preparation time: 15 mins
Cooking time: 20 mins
Serves 6 – 8 persons

SOYA CHUNKS STEW

1 tbsp/14g oil
224g packet soya mince
½ tsp turmeric
Salt to taste
1 tomato, chopped
1 large potato, chopped
1 sweet pepper, chopped
2 tbsp curry powder
Fresh seasonings:
1 sprig thyme, chives, marjoram, rosemary and oregano, all finely chopped

Preparation time: 10 mins
Cooking time: ½ hour
Serves 4 – 6 persons

- Sauté onion, sweet pepper, garlic and potato.
- Add soya mince, turmeric, curry powder, tomatoes, all fresh seasonings, salt to taste and enough water to achieve a gravy consistency.
- Simmer gently for 10 minutes, stirring occasionally.

SPINACH LOAF

2 cups cooked spinach, chopped
¾ cup milk
1 large onion, minced
1 egg
1 large sweet pepper, minced
2 tbsp/1oz margarine
½ cup/4oz breadcrumbs
4 tbsp Ragu sauce
Salt to taste
¼ cup/2oz cheese

Preparation time: 15 mins
Cooking time: 1 hr
Serves 4- 6 persons

- Preheat oven to 350°F/177°C.
- Mix spinach, margarine, cheese and onion together.
- Add beaten egg, Ragu sauce and milk.
- Stir well and salt to taste.
- Add breadcrumbs, mix well and pour into a greased dish.
- Bake for 45 minutes.

PEANUT BUTTER CARROT ROAST

⅓ cup peanut butter
1 large sweet pepper, minced
⅓ cup tomato puree
1 sprig celery, minced
1 large onion, minced
1 cup shredded carrots
1 ½ cup breadcrumbs
Seasonings:
1 sprig thyme, chive, majoram, rosemary and oregano, all finely chopped

Preparation time: 20 mins
Cooking time: 1 hr 15 mins
Serves 4 -6 persons

- Preheat oven to 300°F/149°C.
- Combine peanut butter, seasonings and tomato puree.
- Blend together well, adding carrots and breadcrumbs.
- Salt to taste.
- Place mixture into a greased dish and bake for 30 minutes.
- Serve slices hot.

THREE-PEA STEW

1 cup red kidney beans
2 tbsp of ketchup
Fresh Seasonings:
- 1 sprig thyme, chive, marjoram, rosemary & oregano, all finely chopped.

Dry Seasonings:
- 1 tsp paprika
- 1 tsp curry

1 cup dried yellow split peas
2 tbsp/1oz olive oil
2 small onions, chopped
2 cloves garlic, minced
1 cup lentil peas
1 large sweet pepper
1 tsp salt

Preparation time: 10 mins
Cooking time: 45 mins
Serves 6- 8 persons

- Cook all the peas in a large saucepan for 30 minutes.
- Sauté onion, sweet pepper and garlic.
- Add cooked peas to the mixture and stir in all the fresh and dry seasonings and salt.
- Simmer for 15 minutes until peas are very soft.
- Add ketchup and a little water.
- Taste and adjust seasonings as necessary to make spicy and tasty.

TIP: Any three different kinds of peas may be used.

VEGETABLES

4 large carrots
1 tsp salt
½ cup/4oz brown sugar
2 tbsp/1oz butter

Preparation time: 5 mins
Cooking time: 15 mins
Serves 4 -6 persons

CANDY CARROTS

- Julienne carrots.
- Boil them in a small amount of water.
- Drain the carrots, reduce the heat to its lowest possible setting and return the carrots to the pan.
- Stir in brown sugar, butter and salt.
- Cook for 3 to 5 minutes, or until sugar is bubbly.
- Serve hot.

1 lb mashed yams
2 tbsp/1oz butter
2 egg yolks, lightly beaten
¼ lb cooked spinach, minced
Salt and pepper to taste
1 cup fine dried bread-crumbs for coating
1 egg, slightly beaten for coating

Preparation time: 7 mins
Cooking time: 15 mins
Serves 4-6

GUYANESE YAM AND SPINACH CROQUETTES

- Combine the ingredients except egg and bread-crumbs, and beat until fluffy.
- Shape into croquettes and dip into egg and roll in breadcrumbs.
- Fry in hot deep fat until brown.
- Serve.

STUFFED SWEET PEPPERS

4 large sweet peppers
14 oz can corn
1 clove garlic
4 large biscuits
Fresh herbs & seasonings:
  1 sprig thyme, chive, marjoram, rosemary, oregan and dill, all finely chopped
1 large onion
¼ cup cheese, grated

Preparation time: 10 mins
Cooking time: 25 mins
Serves 4 persons

- Preheat oven to 375°F/190°C.
- Blanche sweet peppers.
- Chop onion and garlic fine.
- Break up biscuits and add to a small amount of hot water. Then strain onto a plate.
- Sauté the onion and garlic, add the biscuits, corn, herbs and seasonings. Add a portion of the grated cheese.
- Stuff the mixture into the large sweet peppers.
- Sprinkle with remaining portion of the grated cheese.
- Bake on a greased baking tray for 15 minutes to allow cheese to melt. Serve hot.

TIP: Any type of savoury biscuits or crackers may be used.

FRIED CORN

4 veggie hot dogs, chopped
1 onion, chopped
2 medium-sized green bell peppers, chopped
2 (16oz) packages frozen corn
Salt and pepper to taste

- Place hot dogs in a large, deep pan.
- Stir in onion and green bell peppers, and cook until tender.
- Reduce heat to low. Stir in corn and cook until tender.
- Salt and pepper to taste.

Preparation time: 15 mins
Cooking time: 30 mins
Serves 6 – 8 persons

SCALLOPED POTATOES

6 large potatoes
½ cup/4oz of milk
1 tbsp/14g of cooking oil
1 large onion, minced
Salt to taste
2 tbsp/1oz of butter
1 tsp of curry
1 cup grated cheese
1 tsp paprika

Preparation Time: 20 mins
Cooking Time: 1 hr
Serves 4 – 6 persons

CHEESE SAUCE

- Sauté onion in a medium sized saucepan.
- Add grated cheese, milk, curry and paprika.
- Allow cheese sauce to cook for one minute.

- Preheat oven to 300°F/149°C.
- Peel and slice potatoes.
- Boil potatoes in lightly salted water with 1 tablespoon of cooking oil for 10 minutes or until partially cooked.
- Put potatoes to cool.
- Grease a baking dish with butter.
- Place a layer of sliced potatoes to the bottom and cover with cheese sauce.
- Repeat step 6.
- Sprinkle breadcrumbs on the top.
- Bake at 275°F/135°C for 30 minutes and serve hot.

BRAWTA

Okra

Okra grows in an elongated, lantern shape vegetable. It is a fuzzy, green colored, and ribbed pod that is approximately 2-7 inches in length. This vegetable is more famously known by its rows of tiny seeds and slimy or sticky texture when cut open. Okra is also known as bamia, bindi, bhindi, lady's finger and gumbo, and is a member of the cotton (Mallow) family.

Okra was discovered around Ethiopia during the 12th century B.C. and was cultivated by the ancient Egyptians. This vegetable soon flourished throughout North Africa and the Middle East where the seed pods were consumed cooked and the seeds toasted, ground, and served as a coffee substitute. It is now seen in African, Middle Eastern, Greek, Turkish, Indian, Caribbean, and South American cuisines.

Okra is a powerhouse of valuable nutrients. It is a good source of vitamin C. It is low in calories and is fat-free.

CREOLE OKRA

- Sauté the onion and garlic.
- Add the green pepper. Cook and stir until tender.
- Drain the tomatoes, reserving juice, and pour them into the saucepan.
- Season with thyme, parsley, cayenne, salt and pepper. Simmer for 5 minutes over medium heat.
- Add the frozen okra and pour in enough of the reserved juice from the tomatoes to cover the bottom of the pan.
- Cover and cook for 15 minutes, or until okra is tender.

2 tbsp/1oz olive oil
½ large onion, chopped
2 cloves garlic, minced
¼ tsp/1ml cayenne pepper
½ green bell pepper, chopped
1 (16oz) can diced tomatoes in juice
Pinch of dried thyme
1 tbsp fresh parsley, chopped
Salt and pepper to taste
1 (16oz) package frozen cut okra

Preparation time: 20 mins
Cooking time: 30 mins
Serves 6 – 8 persons

PICKLED BREADFRUIT

1 breadfruit (not fully ripe)
1 large sweet pepper, finely minced
4 tbsp lime juice
1 large cucumber, grated
1 large onion, finely minced
2 tbsp/1 oz salt
2 tbsp/1 oz pepper

Preparation time: 20 mins
Cooking time: 30 mins
Serves 8 – 10 persons

- Dice breadfruit and cook in lightly salted water.
- Mix the onion, sweet pepper, cucumber, salt and pepper together to make the pickle.
- Put the breadfruit into a large container and cover it generously with the pickle.
- Squeeze the juice of the other lime all over the mixture.
- Serve at room temperature.

Tip: Green bananas may also be used instead of breadfruit.

BRAWTA

Eggplant

Eggplants are round, oblong shaped vegetables that are found in various colors like deep purple, white and lavender and at times even orange. They are available all throughout the year in markets, but are best to be bought between August and October because that's when they are in season. The eggplant, also known as the purple pear, belongs to the family of nightshade vegetables known as 'Solanaceae'. Other members of this family include tomatoes and bell peppers, and the eggplant grows in a way similar to that of tomatoes. It contains some very essential nutrients and even some medicinal properties that are highly beneficial for the human body.

Eggplants are rich sources of dietary fiber, vitamins and minerals and contain very less calories. This makes it an ideal component of low fat diets and the diets of those working on weight loss. Other essential minerals contained in eggplant include potassium, manganese, magnesium and copper. Eggplants are very important sources of phytonutrients, which is obtained from their deep purple color. Eggplants provide dietary fiber in abundance which is essential for regulating and facilitating smooth bowel movements. The dietary fiber in eggplant also helps to lower blood cholesterol and blood sugar levels. One cup serving of eggplant would contain approximately 10%

of the recommended dietary fiber.

VITAMINS - Eggplants contain vitamins like vitamin C and b-vitamins, but they are not very high in content. One cup cooked serving of eggplant would contain approximately 2-5% of the recommended vitamin B1, vitamin B-3, vitamin B-6 and vitamin C. Potassium One cup serving of eggplant contains around 3% of the recommended potassium intake. The potassium in the eggplants is beneficial for those suffering from low blood pressure levels and it also regulates the beating of the heart. Calories and fats are something, that the eggplant contains the least and this is what makes it a healthy component of daily diet.

EGGPLANT CASSEROLE

- Preheat oven to 300°F/149°C degrees.
- Whisk eggs.
- Place breadcrumbs in a container.
- Slice eggplant ½ inches rounds, dust lightly with paprika and curry.
- Dip seasoned eggplant slices in eggs, then in breadcrumbs to coat.
- Fry coated eggplant slices until golden brown.
- Season with salt and drain on paper towels.
- Sauté onion, garlic, whole tomatoes, and add paprika, curry and the soy sauce for the tomato sauce.
- Layer eggplant, tomato sauce and cheese.
- Bake 275°F/135°C for 25 minutes or until cheese is melted and bubbly.

1 tbsp/14g olive oil
2 eggs, lightly beaten
1 cup breadcrumbs
1 medium-sized can
whole tomatoes
1 eggplant, sliced
Salt to taste
1 medium onion, sliced
4 slices cheese, torn
into strips
2 cups/16oz cheese- grated
Dry seasonings:
1 tsp paprika
1 tsp curry
2 large garlic cloves
1 tsp soy sauce

Preparation time: 10 mins
Cooking time: 40 mins
Serves 6 – 8 persons

ROASTED VEGETABLES

2 large beets
1 medium-sized squash
2 large carrots
1 medium-sized onion, chopped
1 sweet pepper, chopped
1 clove garlic, chopped
2 tbsp/1oz olive oil
Salt to taste

Preparation time: 10 mins
Cooking time: 35 mins
Serves 4 – 6 persons

- Preheat oven to 350°F/177°C.
- Peel and chop all the vegetables different sizes.
- Place the vegetables in a greased baking dish.
- Mix sweet pepper, onion and garlic and olive oil together and put over the vegetables.
- Bake at 400°F/204°C for approximately 20 minutes or until vegetables are tender.
- Serve hot.

JAMAICAN CINNAMON PLANTAINS

2 large, firm, ripe plantains
3 tbsp/42g spice
3 tbsp/42g cinnamon
2 tbsp/1oz butter
¼ cup sugar
½ cup water

Preparation time: 5 mins
Cooking time: 15 mins
Serves 4 – 6 persons

- Peel plantains and cut in thick slices.
- Sauté with butter gently to avoid mashing plantains.
- Add cinnamon, spice and sugar to the plantains.
- Add a little water to create a syrup.
- Allow plantains to steep in syrup for five minutes.
- Serve hot.

DESSERTS

PUMPKIN BREAD

1 cup/8oz pumpkin puree
½ cup of milk
1 ½ cups/12oz of flour
1 tsp/5ml spice
½ tsp salt
1 tsp nutmeg
6 -8 tbsp/4oz butter
1 tsp cinnamon
1 cup sugar
1 tsp baking powder
2 eggs
¼ cup water

Preparation time: 20 mins
Cooking time:1 ¼ hrs
Serves 8 – 10 persons

- Preheat oven to 350°F/177°C.
- In a large bowl mix together flour, salt, baking powder, spice, nutmeg and cinnamon.
- Whisk the butter and eggs together, then add the pumpkin puree and water and whisk again.
- Add the dry ingredients and stir until all the dry and wet ingredients form a firm batter. Do not over mix.
- Pour into a greased baking dish and bake for 45 to 60 minutes or until a cake tester inserted into the middle of the pan comes out clean.

OATMEAL COOKIES

1 cup flour
¼ cup milk
½ tsp salt
1 tsp cinnamon
1 tsp baking powder
½ cup sugar
1 cup oats
¼ cup raisins
¼ cup/2oz melted margarine
2 eggs

Preparation time: 10 mins
Cooking time: 45 mins
Serves 6 – 8 persons

- Preheat oven to 375°F/190°C.
- Spread oats in a single layer and bake until lightly toasted for 3 minutes.
- Sieve dry ingredients in a bowl and add the oats to the mixture.
- Whisk egg and add milk and margarine together.
- Mix dry and moist ingredients together. Add raisins and mix well.
- Scoop a large spoonful of mixture and place on a greased baking sheet and bake at 350°F/177°C for 15 minutes.

- 2 cups flour
- 1½ tbsp baking powder
- 2 cups of mashed ripe banana
- 1 tbsp/½ oz grated orange peel
- 2 eggs
- 1 tsp mixed essence
- ¼ cup honey
- ½ cup milk or water

Preparation time: 15 mins
Cooking time: 1 hr 15 mins
Serves 6 – 8 persons

BANANA BREAD

- Preheat oven to 375°F/190°C.
- Cream margarine and honey.
- Whisk eggs and add to mixture.
- Add orange peel and bananas and mix well.
- Combine milk or water and essence.
- Add the flour, baking powder and a pinch of salt to the mixture and blend well.
- Put the batter in a greased pan and bake for 45 minutes.

CONKIES

- Mix coconut, pumpkin, sweet potato, sugar, spices, mixed essence, raisins, corn flour and salt together thoroughly.
- Stir in melted butter, shortening and milk, and mix until smooth.
- Singe the banana leaves on both sides.
- Place a large spoonful of the mixture onto each banana leaf square, fold the edges to make a neat envelope and tie securely.
- Steam the conkies on a rack over boiling water in a large saucepan or in a steamer, for 1 hour or until they are firm.
- Serve either hot or cold.

1 large dry coconut, grated
¾ lb pumpkin, grated
½ lb sweet potato, grated
1 tsp nutmeg
¾ lb sugar
1 tsp spice
1 tsp mixed essence
½ cup/4oz raisins
2 cups corn flour
1 cup/8oz milk
1 tsp salt
8 tbsp/4oz melted butter or margarine
4 tbsp/2oz shortening, melted
Banana leaves cut in 8 inch squares

Preparation time: 15 mins
Cooking time: 1 hr 15 mins
Serves 8 – 10 persons

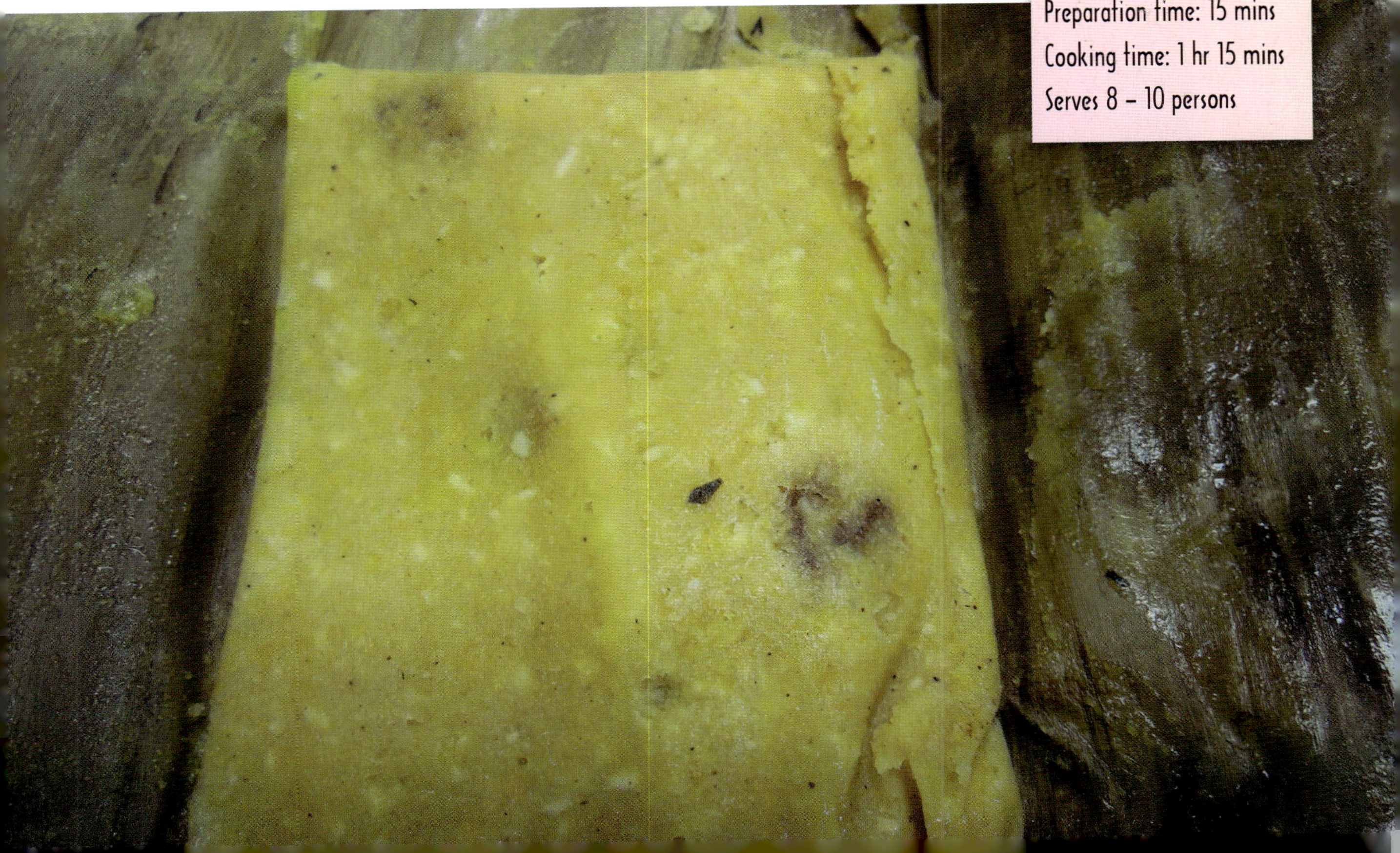

CASSAVA PONE

3 cups fine, dry cassava flour
1½ cups/12oz sugar
1 tsp salt
½ tsp mixed spice
Rind of half an orange
¼ lb/4oz shortening, melted
2 cups milk
2 eggs (beaten)
1 tsp vanilla essence
2 cups coconut, grated

Preparation time: 15 mins
Cooking time: 1 hr 15 mins
Serves 8 – 10 persons

- Preheat oven to 350°F/177°C.
- Mix the dry ingredients.
- Add shortening, milk, eggs and essence.
- Mix well again until the mixture has a solid but not stiff consistency.
- Place mixture in a greased baking pan and bake for 90 minutes.
- Cut in squares before serving.

OAT BREAD (DIABETIC DELIGHT)

- Preheat oven to 350°F/177°C.
- Whisk eggs.
- Cream butter then add eggs.
- Add oats and baking powder and beat with mixer for 2 minutes.
- Coat raisins with flour to avoid sticking together, then add to batter.
- Combine milk, ¼ cup of water, sugar replacement and almond essence then add to batter and mix thoroughly for about 15 seconds.
- Pour batter into a lightly greased pan.
- Bake for 50 to 55 minutes or until a toothpick inserted into the center of the bread comes out clean.

1 lb oats
½ lb/4oz butter
¼ cup water
1 cup evaporated milk
6 eggs
4 tsp baking powder
¼ lb/4oz raisins
1 tsp almond essence
¼ cup/2oz sugar replacement

Preparation time: 10 mins
Cooking time: 1 hr
Serves 8 – 10 persons

FRUIT FLAN

1 cup flour
1 ripe mango
2 tbsp/1oz corn starch
2oz/½ cup margarine
1 orange
1 tbsp/14g baking powder
1 large apple
Pinch of salt
1 cup sugar
3 tbsp apple jam

Preparation time: 20 mins
Cooking time: 1 hr 15 mins
Serves 6-8 persons

- Preheat oven at 325°F/163°C.
- Slice the fruit evenly.
- Rub the margarine into the flour using a fork until it resembles breadcrumbs.
- Add pinch of salt and ½ cup sugar and mix well.
- Make a well in the centre of the mixture and pour in cold water and slowly mix the flour mixture with the water.
- Knead the mixture and form a ball.
- Use a rolling pin and flatten the mixture. Put over a flan baking pan and bake for 20 minutes at 400°F/204°C.
- Puree two chunks of apple.
- Boil the remaining ½ cup sugar and apple puree with a ½ cup water for 2 minutes. Add corn starch for thickness.
- When the pastry is cooled, put the corn starch mixture in bottom of flan.
- Arrange the fruits on the top.
- Use 3 tbsp of apple jam, microwave for 30 seconds or heat quickly in a pan (for about 3 minutes). Add 1tbsp of water to mixture. Strain and allow the glaze mixture to cool for a few minutes.
- Brush glaze over fruits and refrigerate.

TIP: Pastry cream can also be used in place of apple/corn starch mixture.

GUYANESE RICE PUDDING

½ cup/4oz raisins
1 cup rice
2 cups milk
Pinch of salt
1 tbsp/14g butter
1 tsp ground cinnamon
4oz/½ cup sugar
1 tsp ground nutmeg
½ cup/4oz butter
5oz can sweetened condensed milk

Preparation time: 15 mins
Cooking time: 15 mins
Serves 6 – 8 persons

- Cook rice with the pinch of salt.
- Bring to boil, then add milk and butter and let simmer for 20 to 25 minutes.
- Remove from pot and add cinnamon, nutmeg and condensed milk. The pudding should look creamy.
- Add the raisins and return to low heat for 3 to 4 minutes.
- Serve immediately.

GUYANESE VERMICELLI CAKE

- Melt butter in a deep pot on low heat. Add vermicelli noodles and parch it until some of the noodles become brown.
- Add all the milks, extracts, spices and water.
- Keeping the stove on low heat, let the noodles boil in the milk until they start to soften up, add cherries and currants.
- About 15 minutes in, the mixture should start to clump.
- Mixture will look dried out when the liquid is absorbed. If the mixture coats the back of a spoon thickly without dripping, then remove from heat and pour into a dish that will allow your vermicelli to be about 1½ inches in thickness.
- Let this sit out for about 2-3 hours to firm up, or you can put it into the refrigerator to firm up faster. Cut and enjoy.

200g (1 pack) vermicelli noodles
14 maraschino cherries, roughly chopped
¼ cup/2oz currants
4 tbsp/2oz salted butter
½ cup/4oz sugar
½ tsp cinnamon
¼ tsp nutmeg
1 tsp vanilla
½ tsp almond essence
12oz can evaporated milk
3 ½ cups whole milk
½ cup water

Preparation time: 20 mins
Cooking time: 3 hrs
Serves 6 – 8 persons

2 cups/16oz soy milk
1 cup/8oz soy yogurt
⅓ cup/5oz maple syrup
Fresh fruit – banana

Preparation time: 20 mins
Cooking time: 3 hrs
Serves 6 – 8 persons

SOY ICE CREAM

- Combine 2 cups of soy milk with 8 ounces of soy yogurt in a food processor. Mix until smooth.
- Add ⅓ cup of maple syrup to the soy mixture.
- Crush fresh fruit to add flavor and texture to your soy ice cream.
- Add the fruit to the mixture. To get a smoother texture, blend in the food processor. To get a chunkier texture, stir the fruit by hand.
- Turn on the ice cream maker before adding the soy mixture.
- Pour the soy mixture into the ice cream maker and close the top securely.
- Cream for approximately 20 minutes.
- Freeze for a few hours to get a hardened consistency.

Tip: Any fresh fruit may be used.

BAJAN SWEET BREAD

- Pre-heat oven to 330°F/166°C.
- Mix flour, baking powder, salt, sugar and raisins together in a bowl.
- Take ½ of the quantity of grated coconut and add to the mixture.
- Add egg, evaporated milk, butter and almond essence to the mixture to form a dough.
- Knead for about 10 minutes until dough is firm but pliable.
- Divide dough in half and fill loaf pans.
- Mix 2 tablespoons of sugar and 1 tablespoon of hot water, and brush mixture over the loaves.
- Bake for approximately 1 hour.
- Let cool in the pans before removing and serving.

2½ cups coconut, grated
½ cup butter, melted
4 cups flour
1 tbsp shortening
1 tbsp baking powder
1 tsp salt
¾ cup sugar
1 cup raisins
1 egg, beaten
1¼ cup evaporated milk
1 tsp almond essence

Preparation time: 5 mins
Cooking time: 1 ½ hrs
Serves 6 – 8 persons

BEVERAGES

12-15 red hibiscus flowers
1 tsp mixed essence
1 lime
Hard spice/cinnamon stick
Sugar to taste

Preparation time: 1 hr 15 mins
Serves 6 – 8 persons

HIBISCUS DRINK

- Remove flower petals.
- Wash and steep in boiling water with hard spice/cinnamon stick for about 1 hour.
- Add lime juice.
- Strain the liquid, add essence and sugar.
- Serve chilled.

CITRUS PUNCH

2 oranges
1 grapefruit
½ lemon
½ pineapple
½ lb cherries
Honey to taste

Preparation time: 5 mins
Serves 6 – 8 persons

- Squeeze all fruits into a large container, removing seeds and extra pith.
- Blend the pineapple and add the juice to the mixture.
- Mix together with a little honey.
- Serve chilled.

CARAMBOLA MOCKTAIL

4 ripe carambolas
10 ripe Bajan cherries
2 cups sparkling water
Sugar to taste

Preparation time: 5 mins
Serves 4 -6 persons

- Cut carambolas in half and remove tails from cherries.
- Put carambolas and cherries in blender with a cup of sparkling water.
- Strain liquid into a large jug with a strainer or cheesecloth.
- Add sugar to sweeten according to your taste and additional cup of sparkling water.
- Strain a second time.
- Serve chilled.

BRAWTA

Aloe Vera

Aloe vera is extracted from the aloe plant and has been credited with the ability to support health. Aloe is a succulent plant that can be grown indoors or outdoors. Aloe vera is used in many forms for its soothing and anti-inflammatory properties, and has been used for centuries as a home remedy.

Aloe vera that comes directly from the plant is a yellowish liquid. It can be obtained by simply breaking off a piece of the aloe vera plant. The liquid will run out and can be applied topically. The leaves can also be crushed and used as a salve.

The beneficial properties of aloe vera come from the 18 amino acids it contains. It is used to support the natural healing of skin that has been damaged. A common usage is to sooth sunburned skin. Aloe vera can also be made into juices, gels, powders and is often added to products. Aloe vera can be found in cosmetics, shampoos, lotions and many other common household aloe vera products. The many benefits of aloe vera are not fully researched yet.

GOING GREEN SMOOTHIE

2 large cucumbers
1 stalk aloe vera
½ cup/4oz spinach leaves
1 cup coconut water
2 ripe bananas

Preparation time: 10 mins
Serves 4 – 6 persons

- Cut aloe vera stalk and put the yellowish gel into the blender.
- Chop cucumbers and blend with the aloe vera.
- Add all other ingredients and blend to a smooth consistency.
- Serve chilled.

Tip: Other green ingredients may be used.

SORREL DRINK

- Place dried sorrel into a large jug, cover with boiling water and let steep for at least 2 hours.
- Pour through a strainer and add a pinch of salt.
- Sugar to taste.
- Place in covered containers with a few whole cloves, hard spice/cinnamon stick and refrigerate.
- Serve chilled.

1 lb dried sorrel
Pinch of salt
Hard spice/cinnamon stick
Boiling water
Whole cloves
1tsp mixed essence
Sugar to taste

Preparation time: 2 hrs 15 mins
Serves 6 – 8 persons

2 apples
2 oranges
2 mangoes
1 banana
2 tbsp sugar
1 papaya
½ lime

Preparation time: 15 mins
Serves 6 – 8 persons

FRUIT PUNCH

- Blend all the fruits together.
- Add 2 tablespoons of sugar and squeeze lime into mixture.
- Blend with crushed ice and serve chilled.

Tip: A variety of different fruits can be used.

SOURSOP & BREADFRUIT DRINK

- Partially cook breadfruit for about 15 minutes in sweetened water.
- De-seed soursop and puree in large blender.
- Add sweetened breadfruit to the blender and puree.
- Add milk and water slowly.
- When liquid is light and thin, add essence and sugar to taste.
- Serve chilled.

¼ breadfruit
Sugar to taste
1 large soursop
1 cup milk
1 tsp mixed essence

Preparation time: 15 mins
Serves 6 – 8 persons

BRAWTA

Ginger

Ginger has long been renowned for its use in cooking and for its aromatic smell, but did you know that there are also many health benefits of ginger root such as curing nausea and helping with digestion?

Ginger is a plant that comes from southeast Asia, and is now also cultivated in Jamaica and other tropical areas. The ginger herb root is used for culinary and medicinal purposes. It is a natural spice and has been used by Chinese herbalists for more than 2,500 years as flavouring in food and also as a medicine.

Health Benefits Of Ginger

There is a wide range of benefits of ginger such as nausea, digestive problems, circulation and arthritis. Ginger is also known to have the ability to calm an upset stomach and to promote the flow of bile. Stomach cramps can be eased and circulation can also be improved. Ginger supports a healthy cardiovascular system by making platelets less sticky which in turn reduces circulatory problems.

Ginger oil used for massage can help relieve painful arthritis due to its anti-inflammatory properties. Ginger is often included in many herbal decongestants and can help to minimise the symptoms of respiratory conditions, colds and allergies.

Ginger can be freshly grated and used in cooking. It is also available as a supplement which can be taken on a daily basis.

Grated ginger root mixed with diluted lime juice can help to soothe the digestive tract and reduce flatulence. It can be made into oil and used to massage areas of localised chronic pain. It can also be taken in an extract form to reduce inflammation.

When choosing a ginger supplement it is essential to choose ones that contain ginger's pungent compounds. These are gingerols and shogaols and are the ginger plant's active ingredients.

Ginger can be used in extract pill form and the dosage for this is 100 to 200mg up to three times a day. Fresh powdered ginger should be taken three times a day ½ to ¾ of a teaspoon. Fresh ginger root can be eaten every four hours but no more than three times a day and should be approximately ½ inch and peeled. Ginger tea which now comes prepackaged can be taken several times a day. Crystallised ginger can be taken twice a day.

With such a wide range of ginger products available and with the ever increasing benefits of ginger being discovered, ginger or a product of ginger is something that everyone should have in their homes.

2 lbs/32oz cucumber
1 large ripe lime
½ lb/8oz ginger
1 tbsp mixed essence
Sugar to taste

Preparation time: 20 mins
Serves 6 – 8 persons

CUCUMBER & GINGER DRINK

- Blend cucumber and ginger together.
- Add lime juice and mixed essence to mixture.
- Sweeten to taste.
- Strain the liquid and serve chilled.

Tip: Cucumber may be replaced with Carambola.

BEET & CHERRY PUNCH

- Puree the beet and cherries together in a large blender.
- Add Angostura bitters, lime juice and sugar to taste.
- Strain, blend with crushed ice and serve chilled.

2 lbs beet
3 lbs cherries
Sugar to taste
1 large ripe lime, juiced
1 tbsp/14g Angostura bitters

Preparation time: 15 mins
Serves 6 – 8 persons

4 green mangoes
5 cups water
1 cup sugar

Preparation time: 10 mins
Serves 6 – 8 persons

MANGO DRINK

- Wash the mangoes and cut into small cubes (keeping the skin).
- Add the mangoes, water and sugar into the blender.
- Blend until smooth.

TROPICAL DELIGHT

1 cup gooseberries
½ cup sugar
¼ cup ginger, chopped
4 large tamarinds

Preparation Time: 15 mins
Serves 6 – 8 persons

- Dissolve sugar in boiling water.
- Remove tails and simmer gooseberries in syrup and reduce.
- Allow to cool.
- Remove tamarind seeds.
- Puree gooseberry mixture with ginger and tamarind.
- Press mixture through sieve and remove all liquid.
- Strain liquid with cheesecloth and serve chilled.

BANANA & MANGO SMOOTHIE

4 bananas
2 large ripe mangoes
1 cup yogurt
½ cup crushed ice

Preparation time: 15 mins
Serves 6 – 8 persons

- Peel bananas and put in blender.
- Slice mangoes and put in blender, removing seeds.
- Add yogurt and crushed ice and blend until smooth.
- Serve chilled.

CARROT & MILK PUNCH

½ cup milk
½ lb/8oz carrots
½ 1tsp nutmeg
Sugar to taste

Preparation time: 5 mins
Serves 4 – 6 persons

- Dice carrots and cook until tender in sweetened water.
- Blend carrots and milk until smooth.
- Mix in nutmeg and stir thoroughly.
- Strain, chill and serve.

8 carambolas
8 cups water
1 cup sugar
1 lime medium-sized, juiced

Preparation time: 10 mins
Serves 6 – 8 persons

CARAMBOLA DRINK

- Wash carambolas and cut into small cubes.
- Blend carambolas and strain liquid into a large jug.
- Add lime juice and sweeten to taste.
- Serve chilled.

GLOSSARY

BATTER - A mixture containing flour and liquid, thin enough to pour.

BEAT - To mix rapidly in order to make a mixture smooth and light by incorporating as much air as possible.

BLANCH - To immerse in rapidly boiling water and allow to cook slightly.

BLEND - To combine ingredients together with a spoon or using a blender.

BOIL - To cook food in a boiling liquid or to heat a liquid until bubbles break the surface.

BRAWTA - Something extra.

CHOP -To cut food into small pieces using a knife.

DEEP-FRY - To cook food in hot fat or oil deep enough so that it is completely covered. The food produced has a crisp, dry exterior and moist interior once the correct temperature is used.

DICE - To cut food into small cubes.

DRAIN -To pour off liquid from food, often using a colander.

FOLD – To combine a light mixture like beaten egg whites with a much heavier mixture like whipped cream. Place the lighter mixture on top of the heavier one using the edge of a rubber spatula, cut down through the middle of both mixtures, across the bottom of the bowl.

FRY - To cook food in hot fat or oil over moderate to high heat.

GARNISH - To decorate a dish both to enhance its appearance and to provide a flavorful foil. Parsley, lemon slices, raw vegetables and other herbs are all forms of garnishes.

GLAZE - To cook with a thin sugar syrup cooked to crack stage; mixture may be thickened slightly. Also, to cover with a thin, glossy icing.

GRATE -To reduce a large piece of food to coarse or fine threads by rubbing it against a grater or food processor.

GRILL -To cook food on a grill over hot coals or other heat source.

JULIENNE -To cut food into thin, even sticks.

KNEAD - To mix and work dough into an elastic mass. It is done with a pressing-folding-turning action. First the dough is pressed with the heels of both hands and pushed away from the body so the dough stretches out.

MARINATE -To soak food in a seasoned liquid mixture for a certain length of time to add flavour.

MASH - To crush food into a smooth, paste-like texture.

MINCE - To cut food into very tiny pieces.

PARE - To remove the outer layer of foods using a paring knife or a vegetable peeler.

PEEL- To remove the skin or rind from a vegetable or fruit using a vegetable peeler or a knife.

REDUCE - To boil down until the desired volume is reached by evaporation.

ROAST - To cook by dry heat in an oven or open flame as with a spit.

SAUTÉ -To cook food quickly in a small amount of fat or oil, until brown, in a skillet or sauté pan over direct heat.

SEASON - To add flavor to foods.

SHRED - To cut food into thin strips by hand or by using a food processor or grater.

SIEVE - Press the solids, using a spoon, into the strainer to remove as much liquid as possible.

SINGE - To burn superficially or lightly.

SIMMER -To cook food in liquid over gentle heat, just below the boiling point.

STEAM - To cook food on a rack or in steamer basket over a boiling liquid in a covered pan.

STRAIN - To remove undesirable particles from a liquid or to separate liquid from solids.

TOSS - To combine ingredients with a lifting motion.

WHIP- To beat ingredients until light and fluffy. Air is incorporated into the ingredients as they are whipped, increasing their volume until they are light and fluffy.

WHISK - To beat ingredients together until smooth, using a whisk.

VOLUME CONVERSIONS

LIQUIDS ONLY

IMPERIAL QUANTITY	METRIC EQUIVALENT
1 teaspoon	5 mL
1 tablespoon *or* 1/2 fluid ounce	15 mL
1 fluid ounce *or* 1/8 cup	30 mL
1/4 cup *or* 2 fluid ounces	60 mL
1/3 cup	80 mL
1/2 cup *or* 4 fluid ounces	120 mL
2/3 cup	160 mL
3/4 cup *or* 6 fluid ounces	180 mL
1 cup *or* 8 fluid ounces *or* half a pint	240 mL
1 1/2 cups *or* 12 fluid ounces	350 mL
2 cups *or* 1 pint *or* 16 fluid ounces	475 mL
3 cups *or* 1 1/2 pints	700 mL
4 cups *or* 2 pints *or* 1 quart	950 mL
4 quarts *or* 1 gallon	3.8 L

WEIGHT CONVERSIONS

IMPERIAL QUANTITY	METRIC EQUIVALENT
1 ounce	28 g
4 ounces *or* 1/4 pound	113 g
1/3 pound	150 g
8 ounces *or* 1/2 pound	230 g
2/3 pound	300 g
12 ounces *or* 3/4 pound	340 g
1 pound *or* 16 ounces	450 g
2 pounds	900 g